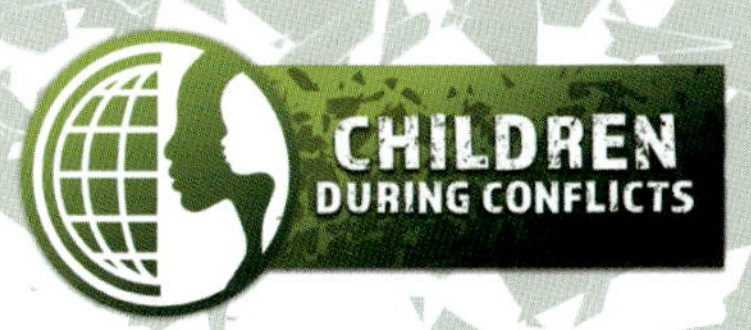

The History of Children and Conflicts

Petrice Custance

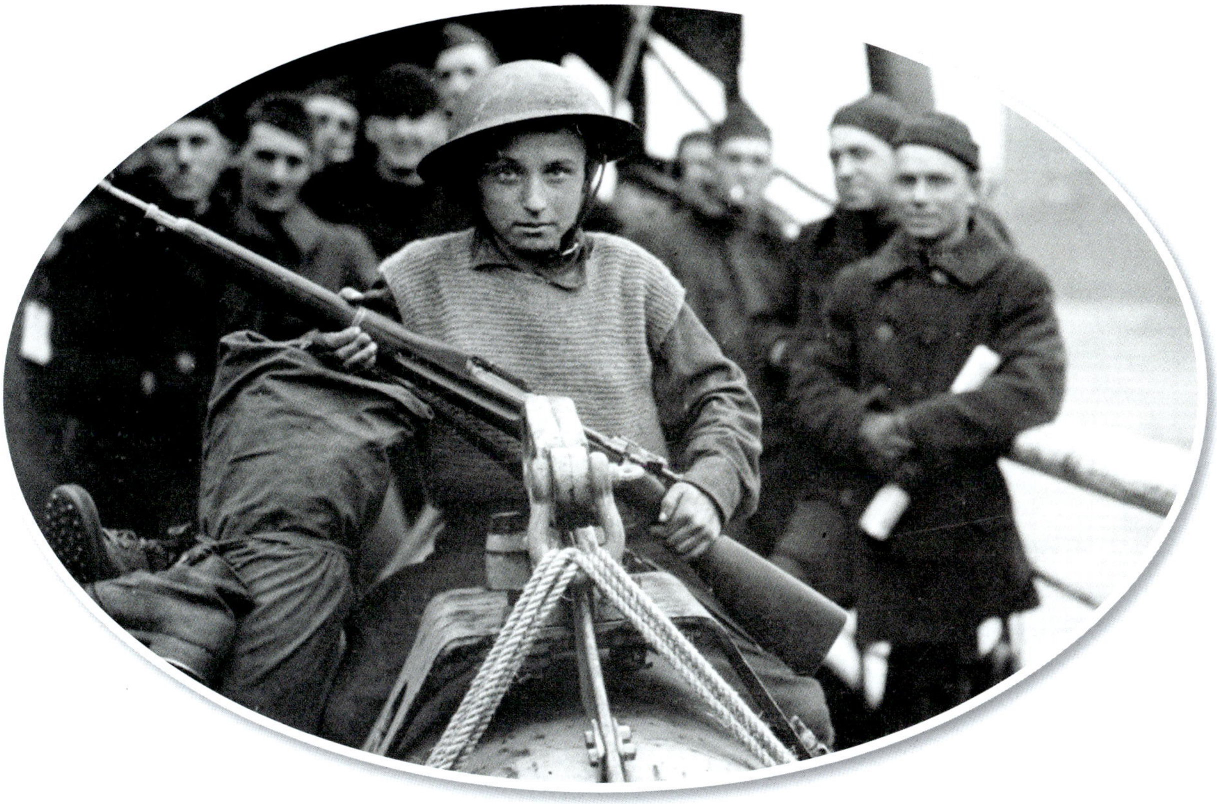

A Crabtree Forest Book

crabtreebooks.com

Author: Petrice Custance

Series research and development:
Ellen Rodger and Janine Deschenes

Editorial director: Kathy Middleton

Editor: Ellen Rodger

Proofreader: Melissa Boyce

Design: Samara Parent

IMAGE CREDITS

Library of Congress:
National Photo Company Collection: p 24 (middle)

Shutterstock:
a katz: p 34; Blake Elliott: p 34; Chris Allan: p 40; De Jongh Photography: p 32; Djohan Shahrin: p 45; Everett Collection: front cover, title page, p 6, 7 (top), 18 (bottom), 22, 23, 42, 44 (bottom); Husam Alqoliaa: p 7 (bottom); laranik: p 35 (bottom); meunierd: p 29; Michael Gordon: p 38 (top); Naeblys: p 35 (top); Ron Adar: p 38 (bottom); Sean Pavone: p 39; Sergey-73: p 31 (top); Shawn Goldberg: p 41 (bottom); Tony Baggett: p 12

Wikimedia Commons:
German Federal Archive: p 27 (bottom), 30 (top); Jrozwado: p 19 (top); Library Company of Philadelphia: p 14; Mbzt: p 5 (top); NorthernFalcon: p 41 (top); public domain: p 5 (bottom), 8, 10, 11, 15 (both), 16 (both), 17 (both), 18 (top), 19 (middle), 20, 21, 24 (top), 25, 26 (both), 27 (top), 28, 30 (bottom), 31 (bottom), 33, 37 (both); Smash the Iron Cage: p 36

Crabtree Publishing

crabtreebooks.com 800-387-7650

In Canada: We acknowledge the financial support of the Government of Canada through the Canada Book Fund for our publishing activities.

Hardcover 978-1-0398-1530-8
Paperback 978-1-0398-1556-8
Ebook (pdf) 978-1-0398-1608-4
Epub 978-1-0398-1582-7

Published in Canada
Crabtree Publishing
616 Welland Avenue
St. Catharines, Ontario
L2M 5V6

Published in the United States
Crabtree Publishing
347 Fifth Avenue
Suite 1402-145
New York, New York, 10016

Library and Archives Canada Cataloguing in Publication
Available at Library and Archives Canada

Library of Congress Cataloging-in-Publication Data
Available at the Library of Congress

Printed in the U.S.A./072023/CG20230214

CONTENTS

Introduction

Ten-year-old Pierre and his little sister Sylvie are huddled beneath their kitchen table. Bombs are exploding outside of their home in a small village in northern France. It is August 1914, the beginning of **World War I**. Sylvie looks up at her brother, her eyes wide with fear. Pierre grips her hand tightly. Their mother is three blocks away at the market. Their father left to fight in the war a week ago. Pierre and Sylvie have no idea if their parents are still alive. The sound of exploding bombs is getting closer and louder. Pierre and Sylvie are alone. They are terrified.

War is terrifying for anyone, but especially for children. Children don't have the full ability to understand why the adults around them are causing such devastating destruction. All that many children know in times of war is that they are not safe and they are frightened.

Nearly every country and culture that has ever existed has experienced war. Based on stone carvings, it is believed the first war in recorded history was in Mesopotamia, or ancient Iraq, in 2700 B.C.E. But **archaeologists** believe wars were fought long before that. Which means there have always been victims of war.

Art from the Akkadian Empire shows archers and warriors fighting in battle. This ancient Mesopotamian art dates back to 2300–2250 B.C.E.

When children live around the rubble of war, it doesn't matter what time period or country they are living in—witnessing war is always harmful.

Chapter One

As Old as Time

It is only recently that childhood has been viewed as it is now: a time when children need special care and protection. In the past, children were often seen as little adults who were expected to do most of the same work as adults.

Children have always lived in adult worlds. But, from ancient times through to the early 1900s, childhood was often short and difficult. Families needed children to work in farm fields or caring for younger children. In more recent times, children as young as eight worked in mines or factories. Schooling often depended on parents' ability to pay. It wasn't until 1870 that all American states had public grade schools.

(right) Breaker boys broke up coal dug from mines to be used for heating buildings. These boys were between eight and 12 years old, and worked 10 hours a day, six days a week. They worked in Pennsylvania's coal regions.

Children worked in factories and warehouses in the early 1900s. They were paid little, but their income was needed to support their families.

War and Children

Today, most children depend on adults for basic needs such as food and shelter, as well as care, affection, and protection. But in times of war, children are placed in life-threatening situations. In conflict zones, children experience and witness violence. They are killed or injured. Somc are forced to fight. Just like children hundreds or thousands of years ago, many must help their families survive conflicts by working or taking on more chores. The **trauma** of these wartime experiences often has lasting effects on children's lives.

Children in Yemen help their families fetch water. Water supplies have been cut off or destroyed since a **civil war** began in that Arabian Peninsula country in 2014.

> ***Every war is a war against children.***
>
> **Eglantyne Jebb, founder of Save the Children**

Child Warriors of Sparta

The harsh treatment of children was a way of life in Sparta. Sparta was a **city-state** in ancient Greece that existed from about 950 B.C.E. to 192 B.C.E. Sparta was a warrior society. Beginning at the age of seven, the lives of Sparta's male children revolved around training for warfare. They were removed from their families and sent to live at a school called the *agoge*.

Some historians believe that the Spartan government, in its quest for a society of mighty warriors, inspected every newborn baby. If the baby seemed sick or weak, it was abandoned and left to die.

Governments bear the primary responsibility for protecting children in situations of armed conflict and in preventing those conflicts from taking place.

Graça Machel,
"Impact of armed conflict on children,"
UN Report, 1996

Spartan children did learn to read and write, but most of their training revolved around physical fitness, strength, and battle preparation. In the *agoge*, Spartan boys faced many hardships. They were trained to withstand hunger and pain, and the boys were encouraged to fight each other. If a boy showed weakness, he was teased and physically abused.

Female Spartan children remained with their families. They also received instruction in physical fitness because it was believed that strong girls would become strong women who would then give birth to strong boys.

Much of what we know today about the Spartans comes from a writer named Plutarch. But he wrote about the Spartans more than 200 years after their **civilization** ended, so nobody knows if what he wrote was completely true.

CONSIDER THIS

How is your life different from Spartan warrior-society children?

The Children's Crusade

The Crusades were a series of wars fought between 1096 and 1291. These wars were led by European **Christians** against Muslims in order to win back control of the **Holy Land**. In 1212, two 12-year-old boys claimed to have had visions telling them to lead a crusade to the Holy Land. They were Stephen of Cloyes from France and Nicholas of Cologne from Germany. The history of what was called the Children's Crusade is mixed. Some sources say thousands of children followed Stephen and Nicholas in this war. Others say they were a mix of children and poor adults.

The Children's Crusade was not an official crusade because it was not approved by the pope, or the head of the Catholic Church. Many works of art that show the Children's Crusade were created hundreds of years later and not based on fact.

Stephen's and Nicholas's groups of children walked across Europe in their quest to reach the Holy Land. However, both groups only made it as far as the coast of the Mediterranean Sea. The children had no training, no weapons, and no money to pay for ships to cross the sea. Some of the children, believing their crusade was approved by God, expected the sea to part for them so they could walk across it. When this did not happen, many children turned around and went back home. But there are also stories of some of the children suffering violence, being sold into slavery, and dying of hunger.

Many people believe that Nicholas of Cologne was the basis for the children's story "The Pied Piper." In the story, a young man playing a flute lures a town's children away with his music and they are never seen again.

Medieval Pages and Squires

The medieval era is the time period from roughly 500–1500. At this time, knights were the highest level of soldiers. Only wealthy people could be knights because armor, weapons, and horses were very costly. But the first step to becoming a knight began at age seven. At this age, boys from wealthy families were sent to live with a knight and serve as his page. At age 14, a page became a squire. Squires often accompanied their knight to the battlefield. If they performed well, squires usually became knights themselves by age 21.

Training to be a page or squire was viewed as an education. Pages learned horse riding, hunting, and combat skills. Their duties included making sure the knight's armor was polished, and making sure that weapons were ready for use. The pages in this artwork are attending a queen's coronation.

PERSPECTIVES

Joan of Arc

Joan of Arc was born in France in 1412. She grew up on a farm and never learned to read or write. At the age of 13, Joan began hearing voices. She believed angels were telling her to lead France in a battle against England so the French heir to the throne, Charles, could take back his crown. At the age of 16, Joan met with Charles. After questioning her, Charles decided to allow Joan to lead their army in battle. They won, and Joan was given a place of honor at the king's coronation. Word of her bravery spread throughout France and she was greeted with cheers. In 1430, Joan was captured by the English during a battle. They claimed she was a witch and she was burned at the stake in 1431. She was 19 years old. King Charles did nothing to help set Joan free.

Joan was later made a saint by the Catholic Church. Today, she is still considered a national hero in France.

I am not afraid. I was born to do this.

Joan of Arc

Chapter Two

Revolutions and Children

The 1700s through 1800s were a time of great change. Large wooden sailing vessels ruled the seas, allowing many European empires to expand around the globe—often waging war. As well, new political ideas were spreading that led to revolutions **in Europe and North America.**

Children had roles to play on revolutionary battlefields—both on land and at sea. Some were made to serve on ships or in land armies. Others lived in areas where war was declared and were forced to fight or survive war on their doorsteps. In 1756, England began enlisting young boys, aged 12 to 14, in the British Navy. Often, they were poor and their parents could not afford to raise them. The navy provided shelter, an education, and a chance to learn a trade, or skill, for a job.

Emily Geiger was 16 when she acted as courier for patriots during the **American Revolutionary War** (1775–1783). Many battles were fought near homes.

Powder Monkeys

Young boys typically served on ships either as cabin boys or powder monkeys. Cabin boys helped the cook and carried meals to the crew, delivered messages, and stood guard. Powder monkeys had a much more dangerous and terrifying job. They carried bags of gunpowder from the lowest level of the ship up to the firing guns and cannons on the upper decks during battle. Young boys were prized for this job because they could run fast and easily fit into cramped areas of the ship.

A powder monkey on a Union ship during the American Civil War (1861–1865)

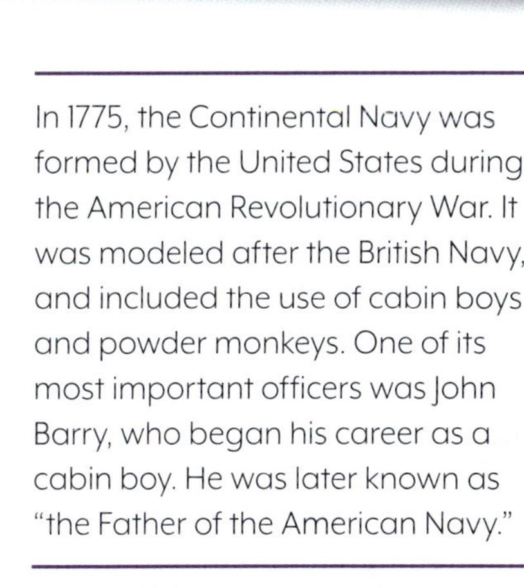

In 1775, the Continental Navy was formed by the United States during the American Revolutionary War. It was modeled after the British Navy, and included the use of cabin boys and powder monkeys. One of its most important officers was John Barry, who began his career as a cabin boy. He was later known as "the Father of the American Navy."

The French Revolution began on July 14, 1789, when revolutionaries seized control of a prison called the Bastille. The prison was seen as a symbol of the monarchy's abuse of power.

The French Revolution

The French Revolution (1789–1799) was a time of violent conflict and social change in France. It affected both children and adults. Unhappy with their government and king, the French people overthrew them both and took control. The revolution lasted 10 years and during that time France endured what was called the "Reign of Terror." This was a period when people suspected of opposing the revolution were violently executed.

During the French Revolution, children witnessed public outdoor executions. Children were also accused of joining violent revolutionary gangs.

PERSPECTIVES

Joseph Bara, Revolutionary Drummer Boy

Joseph Bara became a child hero and symbol of the French Revolution. Joseph was a 13-year-old drummer boy who was killed when he tried to prevent people from stealing two horses. These thieves were counter-revolutionaries, or people opposed to the revolution. After his death, Joseph's story was changed into a heroic act of a child fighting the corrupt government. Joseph was said to be beating his drum when he met with enemies of the revolution. It was said that people opposed to the revolution demanded Joseph declare "Long live the King," and when he instead yelled, "Long live the republic," he was shot.

No one knows which version of the story is true, but Joseph became a hero in death. This inspired people emotionally. He became a hero to the nation.

One of the leaders of the revolution reportedly said about Joseph Bara, "Only the French have 13-year-old heroes."

Children on Battlefields

The French Revolution ended in 1799 when Napoleon Bonaparte took control of France. He was a military commander who crowned himself emperor of France in 1804. Napoleon embarked on a series of conflicts called the Napoleonic Wars (1803–1815). These wars were known for the massive destruction done by large armies. An estimated 6 million people died. The deaths included civilians and children killed through violence and those who starved to death after armies took the crops and animals they needed to survive.

Children also served for all sides during the Napoleonic Wars. Some were drummer boys.

CONSIDER THIS

How did war and conflict impact children in war zones?

In 1815, a 16-year-old British trumpeter named John Edwards sounded the charge that would lead to Napoleon's final defeat at the Battle of Waterloo. John Edwards joined the army at the age of nine.

The American Revolutionary drummer boy in this monument in Savannah, Georgia, is 12-year-old Henri Christophe. Formerly enslaved in Saint-Domingue (Haiti), which was ruled by the French, he was part of the French forces that fought with Americans in the Siege of Savannah in 1779. Henri later become a leader in the Haitian Revolution and Haiti's second president.

Children of the Revolution

Before the French Revolution, there was the American Revolutionary War (1775–1783). American **colonists** were unhappy with the tax they were paying to King George III in England and they wanted independence. Children played a huge role in this war. An estimated 2.5 percent of American Revolutionary soldiers were boys under the age of 15. Some joined willingly out of patriotism, or as an escape from home. Some were sent by their families in place of older family members who were needed at home. And some joined local **militias** as a means of protection from invading British forces.

At home, children often had to take on more responsibilities while the adults were involved in the war. Boys and girls helped with farming, chopping wood, taking care of younger siblings, sewing uniforms, and caring for wounded soldiers.

In 1782, 16-year-old Betty Zane was in Fort Henry in West Virginia with her family when it was under attack by the British. When the defenders of the fort ran out of gunpowder, Betty volunteered to run to her family home to get more. She succeeded, running right past the British forces. The fort remained in American control.

The American Civil War

The American Civil War (1861–1865) was a war between the northern (Union) and southern (Confederate) states. It began because of differences between free and slave states over slavery. Southern states wanted the right to abolish federal laws, keep slaves, and expand slavery into the West. The American Civil War is sometimes called the Boys' War because so many children served. An estimated 250,000 boys between the ages of eight and 18 were active as soldiers or aides on both sides of the conflict. Many recruiters allowed the boys to join. But some boys lied about their age in order to join.

At age eight, Edward Black was the youngest known child soldier of the American Civil War. He served as a drummer boy for the Union army. By the time he was 12, an exploding shell injured his left hand and arm. He never fully recovered from the trauma of his service and died at 19.

> ***As we lay there and the shells were flying over us, my thoughts went back to my home. I thought what a foolish boy I was to run away to get into such a mess I was in. I would have been glad to have seen my father coming after me.***
>
> **Fifteen-year-old Elisha Stockwell Jr. of Wisconsin, private in the Union army**

PERSPECTIVES

John Clem, Youngest Officer

In 1861, at the age of nine, John Clem ran away from home in Ohio after his mother was killed in a train accident. He attempted to join the U.S. Army but was rejected because he was so young and small. He didn't give up, however, and soon became an unofficial drummer boy and mascot for the Union army. His fellow soldiers chipped in to pay his monthly salary of 13 dollars until he was allowed to officially enlist in 1863. At the Battle of Chickamauga in 1863, Clem shot and wounded a Confederate colonel who had demanded that he surrender. This made him famous and he was promoted to sergeant, making him the youngest officer in the U.S. Army. He went on to have a long military career.

In October 1863, Clem was captured by Confederate soldiers. They took his uniform from him as well as his cap, which had three bullet holes in it. This upset Clem more than being taken prisoner because he was very proud of that cap.

Chapter Three

The World at War

The 20th century (1900–1999) saw two devastating world wars and many smaller regional conflicts. Each conflict brought new and more frightening brutality. In each, children were also soldiers and civilian victims.

Children have historically always been witnesses to violence and chaos during conflicts. During World War I (1914–1918), some were underage boys who signed up to fight. Some children were also volunteers who raised money for the war effort. Most, however, were victims of the war who lived where war was fought and were killed or harmed by acts of violence or the struggle to survive after the destruction.

Belgian women and children war refugees evacuated to Holland in 1915–16 after having lost their homes and possessions.

I do not say that children at war do not die like men, if they have to die. To their everlasting honor and our everlasting shame, they do die like men, thus making possible the manly jubilation of patriotic holidays. But they are murdered children all the same.

KURT VONNEGUT,
CAT'S CRADLE

War Orphans

It is estimated that about 15 to 20 million people died during World War I. Another 21 to 23 million people were wounded. These deaths included soldiers and civilians killed in direct conflict, as well as those who died from disease, or famine that followed. One of the effects of this death toll was the creation of a huge number of war orphans. In France alone, around 500,000 children were orphaned. Not only were these children dealing with the grief of losing family members, but many of them also witnessed and experienced violence themselves.

If we are to teach real peace in the world, and if we are to carry on a war against war, we shall have to begin with the children.

Mahatma Gandhi

These WWI French war orphans were sent to an American Red Cross home. The Red Cross sent ships with medical supplies and workers to Europe. It grew to become a major humanitarian organization during this war and others that followed.

Children were often used in propaganda to make adults emotional and encourage them to do things such as join the war effort.

On the Home Front

"Home front" is a term that describes things civilians do while a country's armed forces are at war in another country. On the WWI home fronts, children were an important part of the war effort. Many children joined the Boy Scouts, Girl Scouts, or Girl Guides. These organizations helped with farming and gardening to ensure there was enough food for both people at home as well as the soldiers at the battlefronts. They also raised money, helped in military hospitals, and met trains carrying injured soldiers. Some wound rolls of bandages and distributed flyers. Others lent a hand in munitions factories where bullets and bombs were made.

The Scout Movement was founded in 1908 by military hero Robert Baden-Powell, a Lieutenant-General in the British Army. It combined a military model of training youths with outdoor adventure and survival skills.

CONSIDER THIS

Why might children want to volunteer or join organizations that helped their country's war efforts?

Boy Soldiers

In most countries, the official age for joining the military was 18. During WWI, many recruiters turned a blind eye to obviously underage boys signing up to serve. In Britain, where 19 was the fighting age, it is estimated that 250,000 underage boys were allowed to sign up. At the start of the war, in 1914, there was a great deal of excitement. Boys and young men viewed it as a giant adventure and rushed to join the military. Some boys from poor families joined to "earn their keep" or learn skills that might later get them jobs.

PERSPECTIVES

Momcilo Gavric, 10-Year-Old Corporal

In 1914, at the beginning of World War I, Austro-Hungarian soldiers killed Momcilo Gavric's mother, father, grandmother, and seven of his 10 siblings. Left alone, the eight-year-old Serbian boy found his way to the nearest station of the Serbian Army. He was adopted into the unit and assigned a caretaker to look after him. Momcilo was able to show the Serbian troops the location of the Austro-Hungarian soldiers and participated in the battle that soon followed, making him the youngest person to serve in World War I. At the age of 10, he was promoted to corporal.

Momcilo suffered many injuries during World War I and was awarded several medals. Today, there are monuments dedicated to him and a street has been named after him.

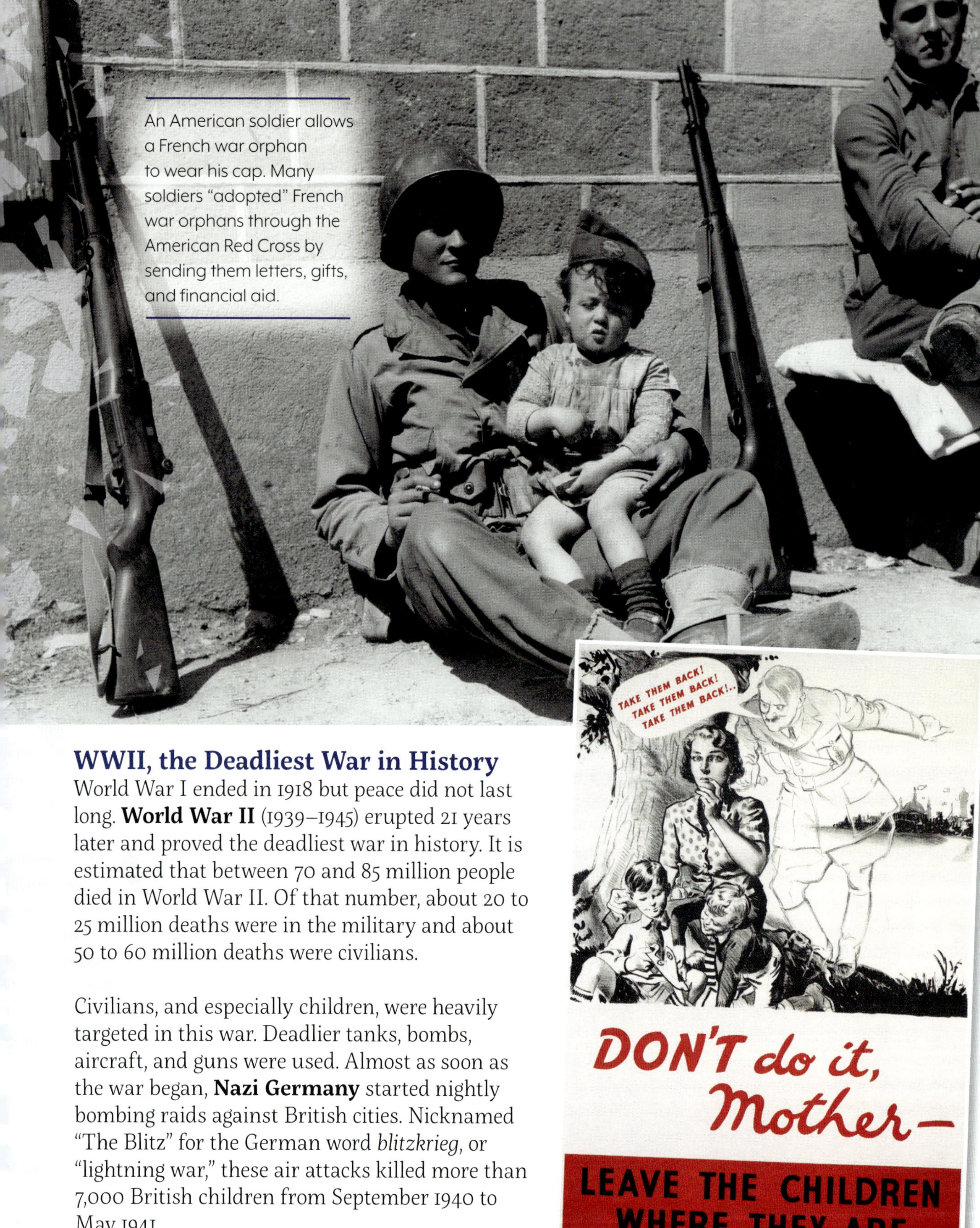

An American soldier allows a French war orphan to wear his cap. Many soldiers "adopted" French war orphans through the American Red Cross by sending them letters, gifts, and financial aid.

WWII, the Deadliest War in History

World War I ended in 1918 but peace did not last long. **World War II** (1939–1945) erupted 21 years later and proved the deadliest war in history. It is estimated that between 70 and 85 million people died in World War II. Of that number, about 20 to 25 million deaths were in the military and about 50 to 60 million deaths were civilians.

Civilians, and especially children, were heavily targeted in this war. Deadlier tanks, bombs, aircraft, and guns were used. Almost as soon as the war began, **Nazi Germany** started nightly bombing raids against British cities. Nicknamed "The Blitz" for the German word *blitzkrieg*, or "lightning war," these air attacks killed more than 7,000 British children from September 1940 to May 1941.

Children in Germany

Even before WWII started, the Nazi government slowly took control of Germany throughout the 1930s. All aspects of life in Germany were affected, including culture and the education of children and youths. By 1936, all German children were required to join a Nazi youth group. At 10, boys joined a group called the *Jungvolk*. At 14, they became part of Hitler Youth. There were similar groups for German girls as well. Some of the children were more loyal to Hitler Youth than their own families, even at times spying on and reporting their own parents if they spoke against the Nazi Party.

CONSIDER THIS

How are children convinced to take part in wars and war efforts? Do you think they all understand what they are doing?

"Whoever has the youth has the future" is a quote by Nazi leader Adolf Hitler. Hitler knew the importance of training children in Nazi ideas so they would grow up to be willing to fight and die for Germany.

Hitler Youth was similar to the Boy Scouts, with an emphasis on outdoor activities such as camping and hiking. The big difference was Hitler Youth's teaching of Nazi ideas, including racism and hate. Many Hitler Youth members went on to serve in Germany's forces.

The Holocaust

The Holocaust, or Shoah, during WWII is one of the darkest chapters in human history. It was a genocide, or the deliberate killing of large numbers of people from a specific ethnic group, race, or nation. Between 1941 and 1945, Nazi Germany murdered an estimated 6 million Jews. Of those, 1.5 million were children. The Nazi goal was to exterminate the Jewish people.

Throughout Germany and in each territory the Nazis conquered as they marched across Europe, Jews were **persecuted** and murdered. Most were rounded up, loaded on railway cattle cars, and sent to **concentration camps**. Upon arrival at the camps, old people, mothers and babies, and children who were not able to work were immediately killed, typically in gas chambers.

Nazi soldiers gathering Jewish women and children after the Warsaw Ghetto Uprising of 1943. The uprising was an act of Jewish resistance to the Nazis who were persecuting, murdering, and deporting Poland's Jews to camps. The resisters rose up to fight rather than wait for the Nazis to kill them.

Experimentation and Murder

The Nazi regime began persecuting Jews, as well as Roma, Sinti, Black, and Slavic peoples, starting in the mid-1930s. Gay people, Jehovah's Witnesses, political opponents, and adults and children with physical and mental disabilities were also targeted for extermination. The Nazi genocide included between 200,000 and 500,000 Roma people.

The Nazis and their wartime allies built thousands of concentration camps. Six were well-known "death camps" where mass murders were committed. Some camps used adults and children for painful, cruel, and often deadly medical experiments. Children were infected with diseases or had limbs needlessly amputated so Nazi doctors could study them. Most of these children were murdered in gas chambers after the experiments were completed.

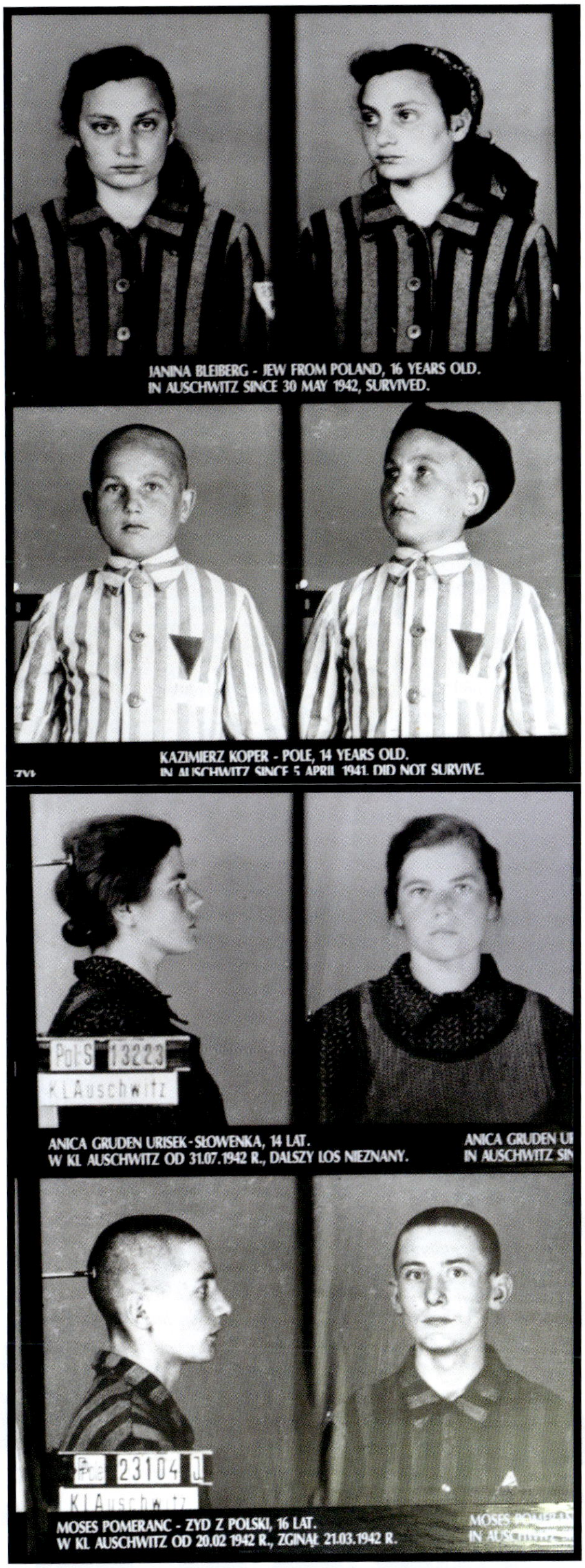

The Nazis kept detailed records and, in some cases, photos of their actions during World War II, including these images of child prisoners taken at the Auschwitz extermination camp.

> ***Only later did I find out that my mother had gone out of the ghetto, sold a diamond and pearl ring to get me an orange. That was the last birthday gift from my parents.***
>
> **Holocaust survivor Gerda Weissmann Klein, U.S. Holocaust Memorial Museum Archive**

Nearly 10,000 children boarded Kindertransport ships to Great Britain where they spent the war in foster care. After the war, many found that their entire families were murdered in Nazi extermination camps.

Kindertransport

The Kindertransport, or Children's Transport, was a series of rescue efforts. It brought thousands of mostly Jewish children under the age of 18 from Nazi Germany and German occupied territories to Great Britain. It operated from 1938 to 1940—when it became impossible for ships to leave occupied ports.

Kindertransport was organized by Jewish and non-Jewish groups and approved by the British government. Some of the children were orphans, others had parents who were desperate to keep their children safe—even if they were not allowed to go with them. The separation was thought to be short, but ended up being forever for most. The children were also classed as "enemy aliens" in Great Britain because it was at war with Germany.

Anne Frank was a Jewish girl who kept a diary for two years while hiding in an attic from the Nazis with her family in Amsterdam, Netherlands. The family was betrayed and sent to concentration camps. Anne was 15 when she died in a camp. Her father survived and later published Anne's diary as a book.

When Bombs Dropped

Japan attacked the American fleet at Pearl Harbor on December 7, 1941, bringing the United States into WWII. The Pacific War was the largest theater, or front, of the war. It was bloody and difficult. It also brought in a new weapon untested on humans: the **atomic bomb**. After four brutal years of fighting, and with the war over in Europe, the United States dropped two atomic bombs on Japan in August 1945. The bombs targeted the cities of Hiroshima and Nagasaki. It is estimated that as many as 140,000 people died in the Hiroshima blast and 74,000 died in the Nagasaki blast. Many were children. Tens of thousands more died in the following years from illness and radiation poisoning.

The Children's Peace Monument is dedicated to the thousands of child victims of the Hiroshima atomic bombing. At the top is a tribute to Sadako Sasaki, a child who later died of leukemia from bomb radiation.

After the attack on Pearl Harbor, both the United States and Canada began detaining and moving their citizens of Japanese descent into isolated internment camps. It was a move rooted in racism and distrust. Many were second- and third-generation Japanese Americans or Japanese Canadians who had no loyalties or ties to Japan. The camps were difficult places to live for both adults and children.

CONSIDER THIS

In what ways are wars a lifetime trauma for children who live through them?

War in Vietnam

Starting just 10 years after the end of WWII, the Vietnam War (1955–1975) was a conflict between North Vietnam and South Vietnam. It is often called a proxy war, or a war between other major powers played out by smaller allies. In this case, the United States and other allies supported South Vietnam, while China and the **Soviet Union** supported North Vietnam. The war was brutal for both soldiers and civilians. Homes and schools were destroyed. Some children went to school at night as it was thought to be safer. North Vietnamese children as young as 13 served as **guerrilla warriors** in the conflict. South Vietnamese children were encouraged to join volunteer movements to assist soldiers.

Many Vietnamese children, like this man, were born with serious harm to their bodies caused by Agent Orange. Agent Orange was a chemical herbicide the U.S. military used to remove leaves from jungle plants. This made it easier to spot North Vietnamese fighters. Millions of gallons were dropped from planes into areas of Vietnam, harming Vietnamese people as well as American soldiers.

Children of War

Starting in 1965, U.S. troops were sent to South Vietnam to help their ally. Some had relationships with South Vietnamese women. It is estimated that as many as 30,000 babies were born during the Vietnam War to South Vietnamese mothers and American soldier fathers. These children often faced harsh discrimination, or unjust treatment, based on their mixed race. Some were cared for by their South Vietnamese families, and some were abandoned at orphanages or lived on the streets.

The U.S. left Vietnam completely in 1975 as North Vietnam fighters took over the entire country. Before it left, the U.S. set up Operation Babylift. This evacuation of about 3,300 orphaned Vietnamese children was an urgent act to save the children. It later became controversial when it was discovered that some of the evacuated children were not orphans. They were forever separated from their parents in Vietnam.

State Violence and Children

Sometimes danger doesn't come from a foreign invasion but from a country's own government. State violence is a term used to describe a government using its authority to cause unnecessary suffering to individual people or groups.

State violence can take many forms, including government policies and laws, police brutality, or even wars and genocides carried out on civilians by government forces. Often, state violence is directed toward ethnic or minority groups, or people whose views are in opposition to the government's. The groups carrying out the violence can include police, paramilitary groups, or armed forces.

Children are witnesses to and victims of state violence in their everyday lives—at school or on the streets of their own neighborhoods.

Unjust Laws and State Violence

Children and youths are especially vulnerable to laws which target them based on skin color, heritage, or culture. From 1948 until 1994, the country of South Africa was an apartheid state. This meant that its citizens were not treated equally. A series of laws forced people to live in separate places based on their skin color. People were punished for breaking those laws.

Even before apartheid, Black schoolchildren were involved in the struggle for racial equality in South Africa. They organized protests and joined youth groups. And they were harshly punished for this. During apartheid, police or armed forces would pick schoolchildren off the streets and either hold them in jail or take them to isolated areas and beat them. **Passive resistance** and peaceful protests were met with extreme violence.

Under apartheid, the white minority held political and social power over the Black majority. The state kept this power through the use of violence.

Soweto Uprising

One series of 1976 protests led by Black schoolchildren was called the Soweto Uprising. The children wanted to learn in their own languages in school instead of Afrikaans, the language of the white colonizers. The police responded with violence. While helicopters flew overhead, police on the ground set dogs on the protesters and shot randomly. An estimated 176 people, mostly children, were killed. More than 1,000 were injured. It took two more decades of resistance to end apartheid in 1994.

Twelve-year-old Hector Pieterson became a symbol of apartheid violence against children when he was shot and killed by government forces while taking part in the Soweto Uprising.

Racial Violence

Slavery officially ended in the United States on December 18, 1865, but it took another 100 years for Black Americans to gain full rights under the law. That 100 years was filled with countless conflicts, injustices, and terror campaigns by white Americans who wanted to keep the nation unequal and segregated.

Between 1877 and 1950, there were more than 4,400 recorded **lynchings** of Black people in the United States. Young people were among the victims. **Civil rights** campaigns and the repeated harassment, attacks, and violent murders of Black children were among the tragedies that influenced the U.S. toward the path of justice.

Lynchings were so widespread that the NAACP made a banner stating "A man was lynched yesterday," and hung it from its headquarters in New York from 1920 to 1938. It was part of a campaign to alert the public and push for anti-lynching legislation.

CONSIDER THIS

Why is state violence and conflict just as brutal and traumatizing for children as the conflict of war?

PERSPECTIVES

Emmett Till's mother, Mamie Till, stands over the body of her murdered son. Mamie made the decision to have an open casket funeral for Emmett. She wanted the world to witness the brutality of his murder.

Emmett Till

Emmett Till was a happy teen from Chicago who liked baseball and playing pranks with his cousins. The summer he turned 14, his mother, Mamie, let him visit his great-uncle and cousins in Money, Mississippi, near where she grew up. Before he left, she told him to be careful. She said that the South was more dangerous for a Black child than Chicago. Emmett would never come home alive. On August 28, 1955, he was abducted from his uncle's house and brutally murdered after a white woman falsely accused him of harassing her.

Lynchings like Emmett's were not unusual. White perpetrators of violence were never held responsible for their crimes. In Emmett's case, two men were later charged and tried for the murder. An all-white jury found them not guilty. The men later admitted to the murder in a magazine interview.

In Montgomery, Alabama, just three months after Emmett's murder, Rosa Parks refused to move to the back of a bus. As a Black person, she was required to do this if a white person was seatless. Parks said that she thought about moving but then thought of Emmett and couldn't. Her arrest later led to the Montgomery bus boycott—a major event in the fight for civil rights.

CONSIDER THIS

Why is it important that children demand their own human rights?

The Birmingham Children's Crusade

Black children both participated in peaceful demonstrations for civil rights and were victims of violent clashes with white mobs and police. On May 2, 1963, more than 1,000 Black students skipped school to attend marches for their civil rights in Birmingham, Alabama. When they were arrested and thrown in jails, hundreds more showed up to protest the next day. Police then brought out fire hoses and police dogs. Still, the children would not back down. This action was known as the Birmingham Children's Crusade. It put the city and police in the spotlight.

(top) Civil rights are the rights guaranteed to everyone under a country's constitution.

The struggle against racial violence and police brutality continues.

The crusade was followed five months later by a deadly bombing of a church. On Sunday, September 15, 1963, members of the **Ku Klux Klan** planted bombs at the Sixteenth Street Baptist Church in Birmingham, Alabama, killing four children. The church was targeted because it was a meeting place for people fighting for civil rights. Outrage by Americans over the murder of children in a church fueled greater support for equal rights for all.

Addie Mae Collins, Cynthia Wesley, Carole Robertson, and Carol Denise McNair—all girls aged 11 to 14—were killed by the blast at the Sixteenth Street Baptist Church. They had been getting ready for a prayer service.

A mad, remorseful, worried community asks, 'Who did it? Who threw that bomb?'...The answer should be, 'We all did it'...The who is every little individual who talks...and spreads the seeds of his hate to his neighbour and his son.

**ALABAMA LAWYER CHARLES MORGAN JR.,
BIRMINGHAM YOUNG MEN'S BUSINESS CLUB SPEECH, SEPT 16, 1963**

Every Child Matters is a saying that reaffirms that Indigenous children are important.

Indigenous Residential Schools

According to the United Nations, Indigenous peoples throughout the world experience state violence and human rights abuses on a daily basis. These abuses include laws aimed at **assimilating** them, or causing them to lose their language and identity as Indigenous peoples. It also includes armed conflict and relocating them forcefully, taking their land.

Beginning in the 1880s and lasting until 1996, the Canadian government set up a school system for Indigenous children with an aim to destroy them as Indigenous peoples. Children were removed from their homes, families, and culture. The residential school system was run in partnership with Christian churches. Children were forced to adopt the Christian religion and forbidden to speak their own languages or practice their own cultures.

Those schools were a war on Aboriginal children, and they took away our identity. First of all, they gave us numbers, we had no names, we were numbers, and they cut our hair. They took away our clothes...we all looked alike.

DORIS YOUNG,
RESIDENTIAL SCHOOL SURVIVOR, TRC FINAL REPORT

Cultural Genocide Aimed at Children

About 150,000 Indigenous children between the ages of four and 16 attended these schools. Many were also abused physically and sexually. An estimated 4,000 to 6,000 children died at residential schools—of disease or murder. Residential schools were deeply traumatizing for survivors, their families, and communities.

From 2008 to 2015, the Canadian government established a Truth and **Reconciliation** Commission about residential schools. Survivors shared their stories and the Commission determined that the school system was a cultural genocide, or intentional destruction of a culture, against Indigenous peoples. The Commission released calls to action, or things that the Canadian government should do to fix the wrongs it has done. Indigenous groups are still pushing the government to act on many of them.

Indigenous youths attend a National Day for Truth and Reconciliation rally in Toronto. They wear orange shirts in honor of Phyllis Webstad, a residential school survivor. When she was six, her grandmother bought her a new orange shirt to wear on her first day at residential school. When Phyllis arrived at school she was stripped of her clothes and never saw the orange shirt again.

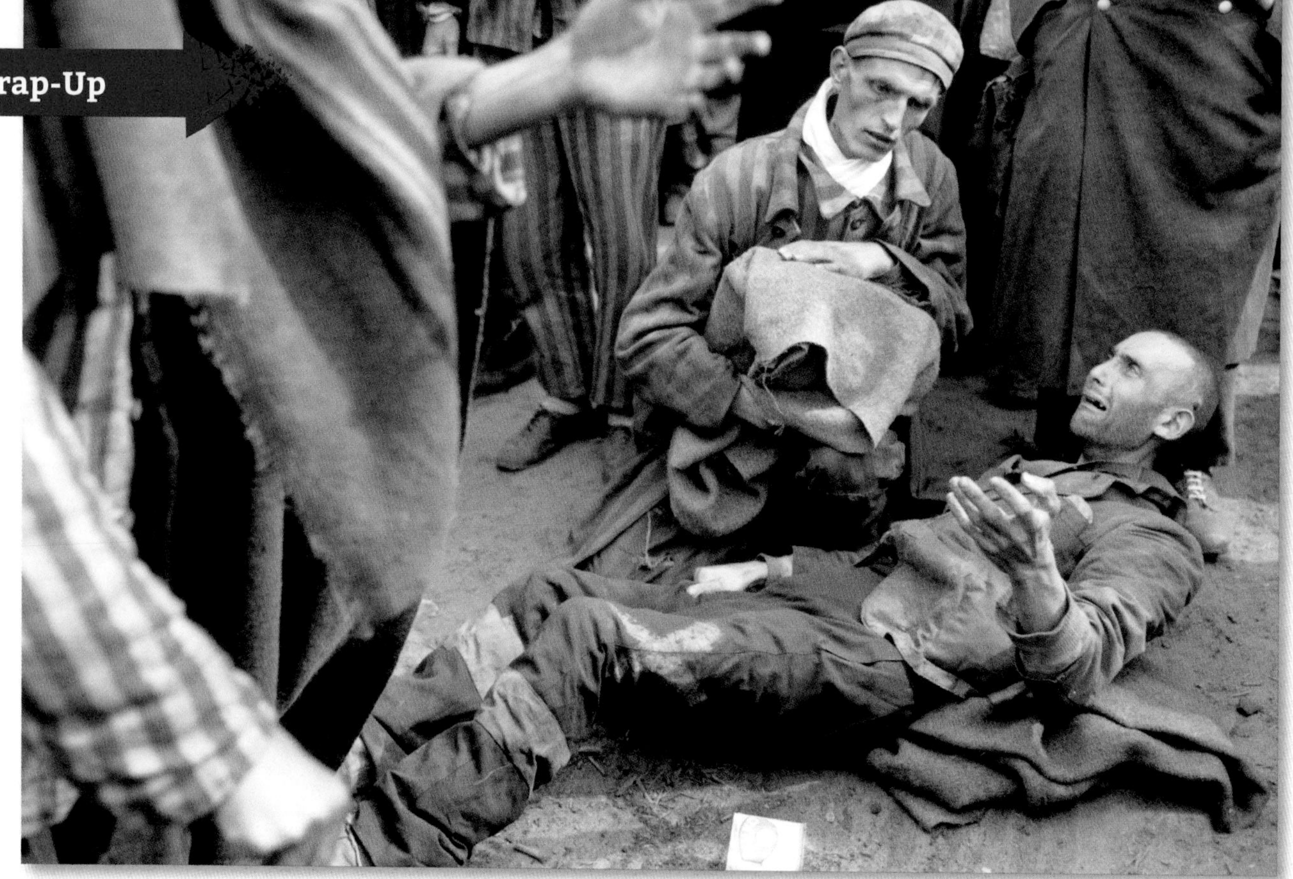

Today and Tomorrow

Adults have a lot to answer for. Throughout history, the wars they have waged and the violence they have shown has impacted children in ways experts are just beginning to understand.

Conflicts harm children, but it doesn't stop there. The trauma of conflicts is intergenerational. This means those who directly experience and witness violence pass their pain on to their own children and grandchildren. Psychological studies have shown children of trauma survivors show signs of post-traumatic stress disorder (PTSD), a mental health disorder triggered by experiencing or witnessing a terrifying event. They also experience anxiety and depression. They often inherit harmful coping or surviving skills that are then passed down to their own children. These coping skills may range from a distrust of others to a need to always be prepared for disaster.

Scientists are studying how trauma can even be passed on through genes inherited from parents. But one study of children of Holocaust survivors showed that parents who could understand and discuss their experiences helped their children come to terms with the history of trauma.

So how do we help children during conflicts today? It is important to support them and give them the tools needed to heal. For example, the Canadian Truth and Reconciliation Commission's 94 Calls to Action are an attempt to get Canada to recognize the "full, horrifying history" of the residential school system. The goal is to prevent these abuses from ever happening again. In other words, it is not enough that the conflict and violence is acknowledged. The parties causing harm must act to repair wrongs from the past and present.

CONSIDER THIS

Can learning about conflicts prevent injustice from happening? If so, how?

Educate Yourself

You can create awareness of how children have always been among the greatest victims of war. The harm done to them is passed down to their own children. This book focuses on just a fraction of the world's conflicts and how children were involved or affected by them. There are many more you can learn about. Ask a librarian to help direct you to books on children and war and conflict. You may have to narrow your search ideas. Frame a question such as, "How do I find information on kids and how they lived during the American Civil War?"

Ukrainian children wait out an air raid in a shelter. Russia launched a full-scale invasion and war on its neighbor, Ukraine, in 2022. Bombs targeting that country have killed hundreds of children in their homes.

British children and their nannies take shelter from bombs in London during WWI. Britain suffered around 50 raids during that war and 550 deaths—at a time when aerial bombardment was new and inaccurate.

PERSPECTIVES

UNICEF, Forged from the Ashes of WWII

The United Nations Children's Fund (formerly the United Nations International Children's Emergency Fund), or UNICEF, works in more than 190 countries to defend children's rights and help keep them safe. It was first established in 1946, just after WWII, to help children and mothers affected by that war. Now UNICEF helps children and women in countries throughout the world. It focuses on health and well-being. Between 2005 and 2020, UNICEF identified 266,000 violations of children's rights in areas of conflict. These included attacks on and abductions of children in conflict areas.

UNICEF asks that governments that support or have influence over warring parties use their influence to protect children.

GLOSSARY

American Revolutionary War A war for American independence fought from 1775 to 1783 by the Continental Army against the British

archaeologist Someone who studies history by examining objects from the past

assimilate To behave in the same way as the dominant social group

atomic bomb A bomb that gets its energy from atoms, the smallest units of matter

Christian A follower of the religious teachings of Jesus Christ

city-state An independent city that governs itself

civil rights The rights of citizens to have freedom and equality

civil war A war between citizens of the same country

civilization The culture and way of life of a particular group of people

colonists People who settle in an area where others already live

concentration camps Mass detention camps where many people were killed

guerilla warrior Someone who fights as part of an unoffical army

Holy Land An area in the Middle East that is important to the Jewish, Christian, and Muslim religions

Ku Klux Klan A white supremacist hate-group formed in the 1860s

lynching A mob murder of someone, often by hanging

militia A group of soldiers who are local citizens and not part of the regular army

Nazi Germany The far-right, fascist government of Germany from 1933 to 1945

passive resistance Nonviolent opposition to or refusal to cooperate with authority

persecuted To be treated unfairly or with hostility because of ethnicity or who you are

reconciliation When groups in conflict make peace and become friendly

revolution Forcible overthrow of government and replacement with a new system

Soviet Union A union of socialist countries that dissolved in 1991

trauma An emotional response to an upsetting or devastating event

World War I A global war that was fought between 1914 and 1918

World War II A global war that was fought between 1939 and 1945

STAY INFORMED

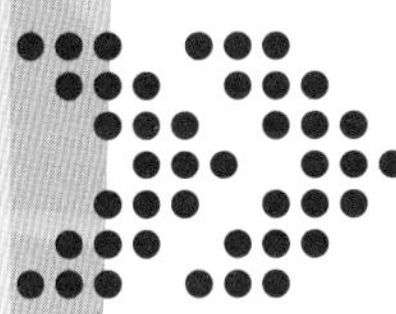

Conflicts in History and You

One in six children are likely to live in a conflict or disaster zone. One of the biggest impacts this can have on a child is the loss of education. We have seen this in other conflicts throughout history. If a child's education is interrupted by conflict, it directly impacts that child's future. What have you learned about conflicts throughout history? What can you do to help children during conflicts today?

1. Read and learn more about past wars and conflicts and how they affect us today.
2. Understand how conflicts and wars impact children.
3. Learn what your country is doing to help children impacted by conflicts.
4. Share what you have learned with other people.

Books to Read

Clark-Robinson, Monica. *Let The Children March.* Clarion Books, 2018.

Frank, Anne. *The Diary of a Young Girl.* Penguin, 2019.

Hopkinson, Deborah. *We Must Not Forget: Holocaust Stories of Survival and Resistance.* Scholastic Focus, 2021.

Websites to Visit

https://www.iwm.org.uk/history/growing-up-in-the-second-world-war

This website by the Imperial War Museum in Britain is designed especially for children. It describes, through images and information, 11 ways that children were affected by World War II.

https://www.historicacanada.ca/content/heritage-minutes/chanie-wenjack

This video tells the story of Chanie Wenjack, an Anishnaabe boy who ran away from a residential school.

https://www.bl.uk/collection-items/impressions-airship-raids-over-london-schoolchildren

This British Library website features essays written by schoolchildren in 1915 about their impressions of airship raids during World War I.

INDEX

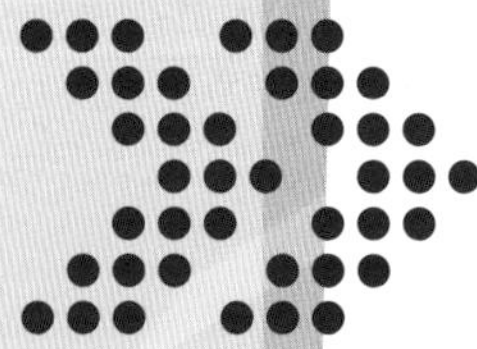

About the Author

Petrice Custance is a writer and editor. It is her honor to share the stories of incredible children, both past and present, who have shown such courage in the darkest of times.